MW01268103

Getting Over A Breakup

75 Easy Steps To Get Over A Breakup

Kate Anderson

Copyright © Kate Anderson Publishing

All rights reserved.
No part of this publication may be reproduced, distributed, or
transmitted in any form or by any means, including photocopying,
recording, or other electronic or mechanical methods, without the
prior written permission of the publisher, except in the case of brief

quotations embodied in critical reviews and certain other noncommercial uses permitted by copyright law.

Table of Contents

6 – Be yourself
7 – Smile
8 – Allow yourself to grieve
9 – Slow down your thinking
10 – Confide in someone safe and let it all out
11 – Remember why you broke up!
12 – Write about it
13 – Allow yourself to be angry
14 – Focus on the things you have
15 – Treat yourself like a friend
16 – Point your energy in the right direction
17 – Recognize your relationship patterns
18 – Don't forget about all the other fish!
19 – Remember that time heals all wounds
20 – Take a break
21 – Think about how your life will be better
22 – Practice acceptance
23 – Keep your wildness in check
24 – Ask your friends & family to avoid talking about your ex
25 – Keep your faith in humanity

Part Three: Get Your Mind Off Your Breakup
1 – Be kind to yourself
2 – Tackle your to do list
3 – Hang out with friends
4 – Keep busy
5 – Start a project
6 – Do the thing you didn't do in your relationship
7 – Sing at the top of your lungs!
8 – Have a movie marathon
9 – Read
10 – Learn something new
11 – Volunteer
12 – Rearrange your furniture
13 – Buy new bedding
14 – Spoil yourself!
15 – Think about the things you didn't like about your ex
16 – Be creative

17 – Spend time with your family
18 – Write a list of things you're looking forward to
19 – Reconnect with old friends
20 – Reflect
21 – Eat well
22 – Go outside!
23 – Exercise
24 – Use daily affirmations and mantras
25 – Take a vacation

Afterward. Life moves on.

Introduction

It's no great revelation to say that *"breaking up is hard to do"* but the fact is, it IS hard. Parting ways with someone you once loved or someone you still do love can be devastating. It can feel like losing a limb. Breaking up can mean losing your best friend. It can leave you confused about the past, present, and future. It can cause feelings of loneliness, desperation, depression, and self loathing. But what's worse is that breaking up can cause you to act a little crazy at times. You might behave in ways that are destructive or irrational. If you allow your breakup pain to rule you, you could end up losing your job, your friends, or your self respect. But it's important to remember from the start that a breakup isn't a death sentence. Your life isn't over, no matter how it feels at the time. You haven't lost everything, even if you feel like you have. You are simply in a period of transition and as scary or difficult as that may seem, there will come a time when this breakup will barely even be a significant event in your past. That is of course, as long as you don't lose your head over it!

For many people breaking up isn't just about losing someone they love, it can also be something quite complicated and daunting. For instance, if you and your ex have a lot of shared possessions, a home together, or children, a break up can entirely change the landscape of your life. If you are forced to see or speak to your ex a lot because of work or other shared obligations things can get difficult. Complications like these can make it very hard to navigate your way through a breakup. But you don't have to be married or to have been with someone for decades in order to experience grief over a breakup. Endings can be extremely difficult to cope with and unfortunately we experience a lot them throughout our lives. Losing a job, experiencing a death in the family, saying farewell to a friend who's moving away, even something other people might find trivial such as losing a piece of jewelry that has sentimental value about can cause serious emotional pain. Endings can feel like an emotional wrecking ball hitting you in the gut with each pendulum swing. It's no wonder people can feel so entirely blindsided by the end of a relationship.

Human contact, love, affection, respect, and playfulness are vital necessities in life. They are some of our most basic needs. Feeling a loss of any of those things can cause you to feel lost and confused. For this reason, when you experience a breakup it's very easy to get trapped in patterns of catastrophic negative thinking. Your thoughts might spin out of control. You might blame yourself for what went wrong and develop feelings of low self worth. You might think (consciously or unconsciously) that without your ex you'll never experience any of those basic needs again. You might think that you'll never be happy again, that you'll never be able to move on, that you'll always hurt. Often when we're swept up in an emotional tsunami, it can be hard to see the light through the darkness. Your thoughts might race from anger to sadness and back again a hundred times a day. You might find yourself acting out of character, drinking too much or becoming reckless and this can be dangerous. It's important to be mindful of your behavior and maintain your sense of self throughout this difficult period. Otherwise you risk acting out in ways that may leave you feeling embarrassed or ashamed in the future.

If you're holding this book right now because you're grieving the end of a relationship, I want you to know that the pain you are in will not last forever. With a little guidance, you can overcome your breakup pain quickly and reclaim your life. There are things you can do to rebuild your self esteem, restore your faith in others, heal your emotional wounds, and get back on a positive track. This book is going to walk through 75 things you can do **TODAY** to start getting over your break up, boost your self esteem, and feel positive about the future again. Written in three easy to follow parts this book covers what NOT to do, how to soothe yourself and recover from your breakup pain, and things you can do to actively get your mind off your ex. Some of the tips in this book will be easier than others, you might have to do some of them more than once but remember: YOU HAVE ALL THE POWER in this situation. You hold all the cards. You are the master of your thoughts, feelings, and your life as a whole. By focusing your energy on yourself rather than your ex, you'll find the days getting lighter and brighter in no time.

Before you begin reading Part One, ask yourself **right now** if you want to be happy. If the answer is "yes" then it's time to get started! Make a commitment to yourself right now to treat yourself well and take the necessary steps toward getting over your breakup and finding true happiness. Let go of your fear and worries. Think about where you want to be in a month's time and picture yourself living a life you're proud of. Get prepared to really care for yourself because soon you'll see that you're strong enough to overcome this and any other obstacles that come your way. You're the one in charge of your life.

Part One: Lose Your Pain, Not Your Mind!

In your post-breakup haze, it's not uncommon to behave in ways that you'll later regret. Sometimes you can be so bulldozed by a breakup that you can't think straight and this can get ugly. The last thing you need after a breakup is to hate yourself because you did something stupid. Now, if you've already acted in ways you wish you hadn't, there's no point in wallowing in it or wishing you hadn't done whatever you did. What's done is done. You can't change the past and scrambling to make things "better" often just makes them worse. However, you can control what happens from this point on and it's important to try to get yourself grounded and clear headed. It might be hard to believe but in the weeks or months following a breakup, *you* can do a lot more to hurt yourself than your ex can.

Think of it this way: there are two people in this situation and you can only control the actions of one of them. Erratic and damaging behavior, self sabotage, self loathing, desperate attempts at rekindling the relationship, internet stalking, seeking revenge… these are all things that could hurt *you* and prolong your pain. And all of these, as well as countless other common pitfalls, are in *your* control.

Don't get me wrong, I am not suggesting that your pain is your fault. Regardless of how or why your relationship ended, your pain is real and natural. Endings are hard for everyone to cope with. Breaking up often means losing someone who loved you and understood you more than anyone else. You might feel hopeless about your future or feel as though you've lost your best friend. You might be experiencing a repetitious onslaught of anger and sadness. It's easy to lose yourself in grief. It's easy to be overcome by it and to have trouble seeing the light at the end of the tunnel. But when it comes to your actions, think of your grief like a drug. It can skew your sense of reality, make you behave in ways you normally wouldn't, and cloud your better judgement. In order to avoid common post-breakup pitfalls, you've got to sober up. This first section shows you what **not** to do and how to keep your post-breakup grief from getting the better of you.

1.) Manage your activity on social media forums.

Social networking sites are extremely dangerous after a breakup. It's all just a little too tempting. For one, it's important to remember that your social pages are NOT your diary. They are not a place for you to air your dirty laundry, bad mouth your ex, or complain 24/7. The only people that deserve to hear about your feelings are you, your close friends and family…and perhaps your therapist! That guy who used to go out with your roommate's cousin isn't interested. Privacy is highly underrated these days. Remember that anything you put online will be there forever. Your pain right now - however serious it is - isn't the kind of thing that needs to define you. Before you put a post up on your pages ask yourself if it's the kind of thing you'll be happy to read over and reminisce about in two years' time. If it's not, find a healthier, *safer*, outlet.

With all of that said, sharing your feelings to all of your acquaintances online is not the most harmful behavior you can indulge in. The real danger lies in that deep dark curiosity, that instance to stalk your ex and find out what they're up to. I cannot stress this enough: social networking is a powerful weapon, it can hurt you! It is up to you to protect yourself from further heartache. If you fall into temptation you may see your ex conversing with someone else and become hurt, jealous, and irrational. The mind has a way of distorting things when you're hurting from a breakup. Often it makes us overthink things and convinces us of the worst possible scenario. You might see a picture of your ex at a party with a beautiful woman and think he's moved on. You might act out. Kick and scream. Cry. Hurt. And then you might find out that the beautiful girl in the photograph is his sister. You might see your ex indulging in what *looks* like flirtatious banter with someone but you'll never know if that's true. The tone within written words can be hard to decipher. What you deduce to be flirtatious might not be. What you think is playful could be confrontational.

This is a big obstacle in communication today and it's not to be underestimated. Reading something the way you want to hear it could hurt you in big ways. Once again, it's up to you to protect yourself.

The best way to avoid getting hurt online is to stay away from social media completely; however, if you can't stay offline entirely, delete your ex (and any other affiliated people) from your friends list so you won't see them in your feed. DO NOT stalk your ex. You're only hurting yourself if you do. Do not look at people they might be dating. Do not stalk your ex's friends. You have to protect yourself in these circumstances. Seeing your ex online will only hurt you. That's all there is to it. You don't need to know what they're up to and you don't need to think about them anymore than you already are. Turn off your computer and pick up a book. Return to social networking when your wounds have healed.

2.) Keep it clean!

Although, it's probably best to avoid contact with your ex completely (especially in the more painful moments immediately proceeding your breakup), it isn't always possible to do so. There are a number of reasons you might have to keep in touch with each other. Perhaps you have children or pets. Perhaps you share a home and need to divvy things up. You might need to meet to exchange belongings or have difficult talks about money. You might even work together and simply can't avoid seeing and talking with one another. However, if you're still in contact with your ex you need to focus on keeping your communication safe with them. Do not talk about your time together. **No inside jokes. No reminiscing. No talking about sex.** Falling into old patterns can be the most painful part of breaking up. It can confuse things, make you hope for a reconciliation, and hold you back from healing. Talking about the way things were will make you miss your ex more. You will long for them more. You will think about your intimate times together and feel the absence of them in your life even more than you already do.

Be especially careful where flirting is concerned. Who knows? Maybe there is a possibility that you'll get back together - anything's possible - but if you do end up back in each other's arms, you want it to be for real. Getting back together on the basis of sex is flimsy and will not lead to a lasting relationship. Flirting creates blurred lines and could make you look desperate: Avoid it. You must remember that you and your ex broke up for a reason. If you have to see them or talk to them you need to protect yourself by creating boundaries. If you find it difficult to tell your ex directly that you'd prefer not to talk about certain things, you can still avoid getting roped into talks of "the good old days" by simply not responding or changing the subject as soon as it comes up. Eventually your ex will get the hint that you're not up for that type of talk.

3.) Let go of "what ifs".

We all can have a tendency to torture ourselves when we're grieving the end of a relationship. We kick ourselves when we're down. One thing that almost everyone notices after a breakup is that they suddenly have a lot of time on their hands. Without having your ex beside you chatting, going out, texting you, cooking dinner etc. the time you spend alone can be long and agonising. It's easy to slip into patterns of unhelpful thinking such as wondering how things *could've* been if only you had of done things differently. Thinking about these fantastical alternate realities is an easy, and very common, way to hold yourself back from getting over a break up.

Indulging in "what ifs" and thinking about how things *could've* gone will not help you cope with how things really are. On the contrary, letting yourself think about things you could've done or should've done will only keep you feeling down and hold you back from moving on. It's natural to wonder if you and your ex may have worked better in a parallel universe but letting your thoughts fall too deeply into something that did not and will not ever happen is a waste of your time and emotional energy. The only thing "what ifs" are going to do for you is knock you down with an onslaught of longing, sorrow, and regret.

4.) Don't beat yourself up.

After a breakup it can be hard to stop thinking about what went wrong. The more alone time you have, the worse these thoughts can be. Even if you believe that the breakup was mutual or the fault of your ex, chances are, you'll still experience a blow to your confidence and self esteem. Feeling down about yourself or regretful about your actions is common but it can also poison you with self doubt and self loathing. You might find yourself rerunning scenarios in your head. Remembering again and again something you once said or did that you wish you could take back.

Once again, it's easy to fall into patterns of kicking yourself when you're down. As you think over things that you wish you could take back they may turn into obsessive thinking about what *you* did wrong. It is very possible that you did something that caused your breakup and it's equally possible that you didn't. But it's important to realise that at this point the reason you and your partner split up is irrelevant. Use it as something to learn from. Use it for your own personal growth. But don't beat yourself up about it. Doing so will not change the past, present or the future, it will only cause you added pain, regret and self loathing; all of which are harmful to your emotional wellbeing. Beating yourself up is a purposeless activity and indulging in too much of it could very well mean that you won't feel confident in future relationships. It might mean that you never seek companionship again.

5.) Don't act out!

Sometimes breakups can make us act in ways we usually wouldn't and that can get pretty ugly. You might find yourself bad mouthing your ex all over town or calling your ex on the phone and shouting at them about all the things they could've done better. Anger is a difficult emotion for anyone to deal with and unfortunately, it's a common emotion to experience after a breakup. If you're not careful you anger could get the best of you. It can and will trump all of your other emotions if you let it. If it's not under your control it can make you act in embarrassing and hurtful ways. It's important to learn to recognise when your anger is getting the better of you.

Anger is perfectly normal in breakups but don't let it dictate your actions. Resist the urge to act out. Screaming and shouting rarely makes an ex want to rekindle a relationship. Name calling and finger pointing will make you look immature and desperate. Writing nasty things about your ex on your social media pages or slandering them to their friends is ugly behaviour that's beneath you. Conduct yourself with poise. Don't lose your mind. If you need to scream and shout, do it alone or in the company of a close friend who you can trust to keep it to themselves.

6.) Assess your friendship.

If you and your ex plan on remaining friends, be realistic about it. Being friends with an ex can be painful. It's difficult to change the landscape of your relationship over night. Most people would agree that taking some time apart until the dust settles is a good idea in these cases. If you believe you can realistically stay in touch without getting hurt or feeling constantly sad or disappointed, go ahead. But if it's killing you to be around your ex and you're having trouble shedding the romantic feelings to you have for them, protect yourself by keeping your distance! Furthermore if you and your ex are going to be friends, you will both have to let go of any anger or resentment the breakup has left you with. It's always possible that you and your might be able to be friends again in the future but you'll need some distance between you for a while in order to let your wounds heal.

In complicated situations where it's impossible to avoid your ex completely (such as couples with children, property, or other shared business with them) you'll need to think about your boundaries and make them clear to your ex. Think about your feelings and make a realistic decision about what you need to feel emotionally safe.

If you find it difficult to be around your ex but you can't avoid it for whatever reason, keep contact to a minimum and keep it respectful and professional. If you find yourself slipping back into old ways with them or you feel like the lines are becoming blurred, pull back and get some distance before trying again. Periods like these can take some trial and error before they're completely resolved. Be smart about it and keep your guard up when it comes to your emotions.

7.) Steer clear of negative influence.

It can be hard to admit it but most of us have a friend or two who add to our negative thinking when we discuss our problems with them. Most of the time, these friends aren't doing this to hurt or upset you and they probably don't even know they're doing it, but being in the presence of someone who is overly negative is something to avoid after a breakup. Whether your friend is entirely unsupportive of your feelings, they rant about your ex in ways that upset you, or they simply encourage you indulge in anger and revenge, it's important to create boundaries where people like this are concerned.

At this time in your life friends that offer support and positivity are more beneficial to you than friends who are bossy, draining, or overbearing. Think of your friends as being in one of two categories: drains and radiators. Drains are people who leave you feeling emotionally depleted and sucked dry. Radiators are people who offer you warmth, comfort, and support. Bare in mind, you don't have to fall out with anyone over this, nor cut friends out of your life completely, but recognizing that someone might not be the best company for you right now could help you recover from your breakup a lot faster. Remember not to make any grand statements or big decisions right now, just try to see a little less of your negative friends for now or when you're in their company tell them that you'd rather not talk about the break up.

8.) Don't talk about your breakup all the time.

Everyone needs a chance to vent from time to time and talking things out with friends or loved ones is a great way to work through your difficult emotions. The important thing about venting is knowing when enough is enough. When the mind is in a fragile state, talking about something upsetting can start to settle in to your mind like a parasite. You might start to feel overly emotional, agitated, or depressed. It's easy to get carried away when talking about your ex and if you get used to doing it a lot you might find that you're not healing very well. In fact, you might notice that you're emotionally "stuck" where your breakup is concerned. You might not be able to get past it or think about anything else. Negative affirmations are dangerous. Try to recognize when it's time to stop talking about the breakup and move on to other things. If you find this particularly difficult (many people do) then ask a friend to put a limit on how much you talk about it or set a timer for a reasonable amount of time to talk about it. When the timer goes off change the topic.

9.) Don't worry about your ex.

If you were the caretaker in your relationship you'll have some habit breaking to do. If you were the one in charge of things like paying the bills, running errands, cooking dinner, etc, you might find yourself worrying about your ex a lot. Feeling a genuine concern for someone else isn't necessarily a bad thing but in this respect it's probably something that you should stop. Now is a time for you to prioritize your needs and take care of yourself. Your ex is capable of doing things on their own. They can get their own food and do their own laundry. They can navigate the world on their own. If they aren't doing well, that isn't your responsibility. It doesn't reflect on you. Try to remember that. When you're used to taking care of your ex in certain respects, it can be hard to let go of that control and concern. Remind yourself that you are the one who needs to benefit from your concern right now. Give yourself a break and focus on yourself.

10.) Beware the rebound.

When you first break up with your partner it's natural to look for a "replacement" of some type (even unconsciously so). This might mean seeking out a new relationship that's purely sexual or it might mean jumping into another serious relationship straight away.

Rebounds can get complicated and often we don't know we're rebounding when we are. The important thing to remember where rebounds are concerned is to honest with yourself and your new lover. If your rebound relationship is only about sex be honest and open about that with the other person. Being in pain from a breakup is not an excuse to put someone else in pain by being dishonest or vague about your intentions with them. Rebounds that are more emotionally intense can get ugly. It can be very hard to see what's really going on when you find yourself rapidly attached to a new person.

Relationships that start too soon after a breakup might not be all they seem. If you recognize that you are jumping into a new relationship too quickly try to slow things down until you can think clearly about what's going on. It can take a while to fully recover from a breakup and jumping into a new relationship before that process is over could end up causing you further upset in the long run. A good rule of thumb to live by is that if you think you're in love and you've only been with your new partner for a matter of weeks, it would be wise to slow it down.

11.) Be careful with alcohol.

Drinking too much can have some pretty serious effects on your mood, your behavior, and your overall wellbeing. Drinking is an easy way to avoid dealing with your problems, thus extending your grieving period. Alcohol can also wreak havoc on your sleep patterns and immune system leaving you tired and burnt out. But perhaps even more importantly, alcohol lowers your inhibitions meaning you're more likely to do erratic things such as indulging in reckless or dangerous behavior or making irrational calls / texts / emails to your ex. When it comes to drinking after a break up try to keep it sane, social and stay away from the phone! The last thing you need right now is negative attention, shame, or increased anxiety.

12.) Avoid making big decisions.

Breakups can take some time to get over and while you're recovering from one you might feel the need for a whole body overhaul. You might feel the desire to change everything in your life all at once. This is often just a mask people put on to run away from their problems. Your grieving mind needs stability and time to heal, so this is not the time to decide to quit your job, move to Alaska, or adopt a chimpanzee. It is natural to feel the need for drastic change but try not to rush into anything. Keep yourself in the present and face your feelings in the here and now. If you feel the need for change, often simply getting a new hairdo will suffice.

13.) Avoid the blame game.

It's easy to get swept away in anger and fighting during a breakup. Even if you're not speaking directly to your ex, you might find yourself talking to your friends about whose "fault" it was. For some people that means blaming their ex for everything. For others, it means blaming themselves. Whatever the case is, the blame game is ugly and fruitless. It leads to purposeless ruminating and only reiterates your negative feelings. Place your focus on healing and what you can do in the future to grow past this difficult time. Meditate on what this relationship has taught you and how you can move positively into the next phase of your life. Placing blame keeps your thoughts and emotions rooted in the past. The goal is to move forward.

14.) Avoid making grand statements.

When big things happen in your life, it's common to catastrophize them as well as most other things in your life. You blow things up in your head and (often unknowingly) give them power over you. A breakup can shake the foundations your life is built upon. It can rattle your self esteem and your confidence in yourself. Around these times people can get into habits of making grand statements about themselves, their lives, or the world in general. Saying things like "I'm bad at relationships.", "I'm different from other people", "I'll never be happy", "The world is a miserable place and I'm an outcast" etc. are negative affirmations and, unsurprisingly, the more you say them, the more you come to believe them.

Yes, sometimes it can feel like things never go your way. Sometimes it feels like the whole world is out to get you. It feels that way for everyone at some time or another. But life is long and you have to persevere. This is *your* life. You have the power to make it what you want it to be. You can seek out opportunities. You can take risks. You can continue living. This is not the end of life, it is merely the closing of a chapter. You can keep learning and growing. This breakup might be an experience that you will always remember but it won't be one that always hurts. This isn't the end of the road, it's just somewhere in the middle.

15.) Don't think about what your ex is doing.

In the weeks and months immediately following a breakup it can be extremely hard to forget about what your ex is up to. You probably know when they're likely to be in work and a few other regular obligations but when it comes to other things you won't. These are the things you have to be really careful about. Wondering where where your ex is, who they might be talking to, and what they're doing can send you into fits of panic, rage, and sadness because chances are, you're imagining the worst. Once again, it must be said that you really have to protect yourself. It's important to be able to recognize when you're thoughts are heading into upsetting and destructive territories so you can stop them before they get the better of you. If you allow destructive thought cycles to happen you're likely to become paranoid and deeply unhappy. Imagining your ex doing things that you find painful will not help you get over anything, rather they'll keep you rooted in paranoia and negativity.

Remember, this isn't about your ex anymore. It's about taking care of you. Don't go down that rabbit hole. Yes, it will be very difficult to take your mind off you ex. There will be times when you feel plagued with memories, flashbacks, and longing, but wondering what they're up to will not serve you well. As soon as you recognize yourself wondering about your ex's whereabouts tell yourself "no". Distract yourself with something else. Put on a funny movie. Phone a friend and have them tell you about their day. Read. Do anything that can direct your attention away from the thing that can hurt you. And whatever you do in these instances, don't look for trouble: NEVER go snooping on social media pages.

16.) Don't fight your feelings.

Experiencing difficult emotions is a very challenging part of life. When you feel sadness, longing, anger, confusion, fear, anxiety and any other common emotion attached to breakups, it's natural to want them to disappear as soon as humanly possible. No one enjoys feeling down in the dumps. However, it's important to listen to your feelings and allow yourself to express them. Keeping them balled up inside or acting like you're absolutely fine because you don't want to appear vulnerable in front of other people could prolong your sadness and make you feel isolated and alone. It's okay to cry from time to time and it's okay to acknowledge your feelings when in the company of others.

We all need to put on a "brave face" in certain situations but you don't need to pretend *everywhere* you go. Your friends, family, and coworkers will understand if you're not feeling in top form straight after your relationship has ended. Admitting you're not feeling the best won't make people think any less of you and if they do, they're probably not the type of people you should be around right now. Allow yourself to feel your feelings. Acknowledge them and then let them fade away. You will recover much quicker this way than you would otherwise.

17.) Avoid calling this a "failed relationship".

One common pitfall a lot of people succumb to in their post-breakup days is referring to this (and other past relationships) as a "failed relationship". This is one of those negative mantras that you need to avoid at this time. Attaching the word "failure" to your current state of mind is not going to serve you well. It will make you feel helpless and hopeless. It will drag your self esteem into the gutter and rob you of your self confidence. This relationship and your other past relationships were not failures. Each of them gave you something. The fact that a relationship has ended does not mean it was worthless or a waste of time. If you felt happiness, security, and affection at any time with your ex, that is a *good* thing that's worth remembering. If you learned and grew as a person, your relationship was *not* a failure, it was a valuable learning experience. Sharing something special with another person is a good thing regardless of if it lasts forever. It may not look like a storybook romance but breaking up doesn't have to nullify all the good things you and your ex shared.

18.) Don't chase your ex.

Generally speaking, trying to get back with your ex is a bad idea. Of course there will always be an exception to this rule (some people breakup in a fit of fear or irrational anxiety that can later resolve itself) but the vast majority of breakups are for good. First of all, it's important to remember that you and your partner broke up for a reason, even if it wasn't your choice to do so. Sometimes the reasons for a breakup aren't as big as someone lying or cheating. Sometimes they're much more subtle and that can be confusing. Maybe your ex wasn't emotionally ready for a relationship, maybe they have some deep rooted issues, or maybe they're just fickle.

Whatever the case, the relationship is over now. The sooner you accept that, the sooner you'll recover from it. Running after your ex doesn't make you look particularly attractive and it'll likely end in feelings of rejection and angst. Chasing your ex can make you look desperate, unhinged, or irrational. Calling your ex, texting them, contacting them on social media, and emailing them must be off limits for a while. Showing up on their doorstep or lurking outside their house is also off limits. Sending letters and gifts is off limits. You get the picture. Accept the power you have and that you don't have. You cannot change this situation. You CAN change how you react to it and how you behave. If you and your ex are the exception to the rule and truly are meant to be, let it happen naturally. Just don't wait around too long.

19.) Avoid looking for information you KNOW will hurt you.

So much about getting over a breakup is about protecting yourself. It's up to you to avoid doing things that threaten your emotional wellbeing. This is most easily represented in avoiding social media but there are many other things to avoid if you want to stay safe. When talking to other people (your friends or you ex's friends) don't ask about your ex! If someone tells you they ran into your ex or they have some juicy gossip about them, tell them you're not interested and change the subject. Be firm about it. The fact is, anything your ex is doing can be twisted up in your head and turned into a weapon for you to hurt yourself with. Having someone tell you they saw your ex with another person at a bar could easily become misconstrued if you're particularly fragile right now.

You could easily start thinking that your ex has moved on and that their half way to the alter with someone new! Seeking out information about your ex will only hurt you in the end. Looking at pictures of them online will do the same. Protecting yourself by avoiding these things will help you recover faster. If you have to meet up with your ex to exchange belongings or to discuss logistical matters, avoid doing so when you're feeling fragile or low. If you know that being around your ex will hurt ask a friend or relative to go on your behalf or postpone the meeting until you're feeling stronger.

20.) Don't let your ex have power over you.

No one on earth should be allowed to control your thoughts or emotions. No one should have the power to weaken you or make you doubt yourself. If you have been in a relationship with someone who deflects negativity onto you a lot; for instance, someone who never admits when they're at fault or always blames other people for their own shortcomings; recognize this pattern and start shielding yourself from it. People who regularly manipulate your emotions can be very difficult to deal with, even if they don't know that's what they're doing to you. Emotional manipulation can fly under the radar in relationships. One partner might regularly make jokes about the other with hurtful and supposedly "sarcastic" comments. They might mock you when you feel good about something you've achieved. Emotionally manipulative people can be very jealous and controlling. They are also very good at making you feel guilty when you have nothing to feel guilty about.

One of the most common forms of emotional manipulation people use is creating a "disclaimer" at the start of a relationship so that when things go wrong they won't be at fault. They give you warnings like, "I'm not good at relationships." so that during the breakup they can get away with saying things like "I warned you. You should've listened to me.", i.e. "This is all on you. You're the one that chose to be with ME." If you've been with someone like this, a breakup can be a minefield where your self esteem is concerned. It's important to tell yourself regularly that this person is manipulating you and that you are not at fault despite what they say. If someone tells you they're "not good at relationships" or they insist on saying that the two of you aren't actually *in* relationship despite the fact that you obviously are, they're doing this because they're a coward and they're afraid of being at fault when they eventually hurt you. They're putting the blame on you before it even happens. If someone has had power over you for a long time (even without you realizing it) it will take practice to build up a defence against them. Remind yourself regularly that no one should be allowed to have power over your emotions.

21.) Do NOT seek revenge!

Feel like getting back at your ex for all the ways they've hurt you? Don't. Keep your playground antics to yourself. No matter what horrible things your ex did you to, getting back at them won't solve a thing. Don't throw eggs at your ex's bedroom window, don't paintball their car, and DO NOT sleep with their friends and family.

Revenge is ugly and purposeless. It might make you feel some sense of relief at the time but, chances are it will make you appear pretty undignified to those around you. If you're tempted to seek revenge, think about how you're going to feel the day after you do it. Is this how you want to present yourself? What does this behavior say about you? Ask yourself why you want to seek revenge. What do you intend to accomplish with it? Is it realistic to suppose that lashing out will make you feel better in the long term? Probably not. Two wrongs don't make a right. If someone has hurt you, hurting them back will probably only hurt you more in the long run. Maintain your dignity and self respect.

22.) Don't rehash old arguments.

Leave the past in the past! Going over upsetting things that happened between you and your ex will not solve a thing. It will only upset you more. If you had an argument (or many arguments) with your ex that are still niggling at you, accept that it happened and let it go. Ask yourself if you want to *win* the argument or if you want it to stop. What is this argument doing for you? What is it doing against you? Chances are, if you and your ex couldn't come to an agreement on something when you were still together, you're not going to come to one now. Winning the argument is no longer relevant at this stage. Don't get in contact with your ex and bring it up again. Don't talk to your friends about it again. Don't let yourself ruminate about it. It happened and now it exists in the past. Leave it there.

Bringing up negative things that happened before, during, or after your breakup won't do anything positive for you. All it will do is keep you rooted in the past, drowning in negativity. Remember: the goal is to accept and recover from your breakup, not to get closure on every disagreement the two of you ever had.

23.) Don't try to make your ex jealous.

Similar to seeking revenge, attempting to make your ex feel jealous is childish and ugly behavior. Posting pictures of your wild nights on your social media pages for the purpose of hurting or embarrassing your ex is undignified and cringeworthy. Flirting with other people in the hopes of having your ex find out about it is a waste of time. Telling your ex or their friends about how incredible and fun your new life is or bragging about how much "action" you're getting can make you look desperate and pitiful. If you see yourself behaving in these ways, ask yourself what your behavior is achieving. Chances are it's not achieving anything other than wasted effort and lost time. Take the focus away from your ex and concentrate on yourself.

24.) Stay away from "special" places.

Revisiting places that remind you of your ex of is a bad idea, whether the memories are fond or painful. Visiting the place you shared your first kiss or walking by a place where the two of you once had an explosive argument is bound to cause you pain right now. The aim of the game is to spare yourself added pain by avoiding reminders of your ex. You will have enough reminders popping into your head throughout the days without actively seeking them. Going to a beach where you once watched the sunrise together is NOT going to make you feel better. Wandering the isles of a grocery store where you had a giggle fit over something only the two of you would ever laugh at is NOT a good idea. If possible, avoid these places altogether.

Consider them off limits until it no longer hurts to be there. Go out of your way to avoid them if you have to. It's going to take a while until you start feeling clear headed again, don't torture yourself!

25.) Don't take bad advice.

If you have a lot of supportive friends and family you're probably going to be forced to listen to a TON of advice following your breakup. Be careful about choosing which advice is good and which isn't. It's great to have people supporting you during this time and having a shoulder to cry on is necessary right now. It's important to remember that your friends and family don't want to cause you any harm but when it comes to your breakup they've probably got an opinion and they won't be afraid to share it. Friends can be overly critical and passionate when it comes to your change in circumstance.

Keep your head on straight. If someone is leading you down a destructive path of revenge and wild nights out, it's usually best to say "no thanks". If they're pushing you to get back together with your ex or start dating other people straight away, make sure you think about those things when you're feeling level headed and make a decision on your own time. If you're finding your friends and family particularly overbearing, tell them that you're not asking for advice or avoid talking about the breakup with them completely.

Part Two: Place the focus on YOU.

Now that you're being extra careful about things *not* to do, it's time to start putting some positive practices in place. Getting over your ex isn't going to be easy but there are a ton of things you can do to keep your thoughts from drifting into negative territory and protect yourself from unexpected pangs of breakup pain. Remember: Your grief will eventually go away. You will not feel like this forever. Soon you will find yourself in a brand new place in life; one that is exciting, intriguing, and fulfilling. On the grand scale of your life, this breakup is no more than a blip and it's important to keep that perspective at the front of your mind. Yes, it feels big right now. Yes, it may be all you're capable of thinking about right now.

Yes, you may be in a state of devastation but this will pass and you will be on the other side of it in no time. One of the great things about life is that time marches on no matter what is happening in our individual lives. We have all felt pain before and most of us will feel it again. But we have also felt joy, exuberance, and vitality before and those feelings will also return to us again. You will laugh again. You will find yourself free of longing again. And eventually this breakup will be a speck of dust in your past.

In order to get through these hard times as quickly as possible, don't forget that you're the one in charge. You get to choose how to compose yourself. You have the choice between protecting yourself from pain or wallowing in it. You might not be able to change what caused your breakup and you can't control your ex but you can control yourself! Below, I have listed 25 things you can do to help keep your emotional head above water. These include ways you can protect yourself from pain as well as ways to eventually overcome it. Be committed to yourself and your wellbeing throughout this time in your life. You deserve it!

1.) Delete daily reminders off your phone and computer.

One of the most effective things you can do when struggling after a breakup is to shield yourself from unnecessary daily reminders of your ex. You might feel as though everywhere you look you see your ex, and because of that you may find yourself obsessively thinking about them and dwelling on times gone by. Certain things will always remind you of your relationship but there are measures you can take to lessen them. Firstly, when you use your mobile phone throughout each day the last thing you need is a picture, email, or a text message bringing you down. If you have photos of your ex on your phone (or photos they took of you) delete them so you don't accidentally see them every time you use your phone. Delete all text messages from your ex too. Seeing their name every time you compose a text message is going to sting. If you feel too attached to let go of your past "conversations" transfer them onto your computer and store them in a hidden folder that you won't look at until you're ready to let go of them for good.

The same applies for emails. Most importantly, don't let yourself read messages from your ex over and over. Don't try to "decifer" what they really meant when they said "…". Let all of that go. It's over now. It doesn't matter what they meant in that conversations and it doesn't matter if they know what *you* meant. Ruminating about things like this will only keep you rooted in anger, disappointment, confusion, and sadness. Accept that you cannot change anything that you once shared with your ex (good or bad) and do what you can to protect yourself *now*.

2.) Get rid of things that evoke memories.

Just like the pictures, texts, and emails you've now deleted from your mobile and computer, having reminders of your ex around your house, in your drawers, on your walls, in your car, on your desk, etc, is not good for you right now. Conduct an exorcism by getting rid of these reminders stat! Anything that reminds you of your ex has to go. This could be things like pictures and letters or obscure things you shared an inside joke about. Have a particular pair of pajamas that make you think of your ex? Throw them out. Bed sheets from a wild night you'll never forget? Buy new ones. Have a book they lent you? Say goodbye.

You must protect yourself from these reminders whether they evoke positive memories or negative ones. Positive memories could lead to false hope, regret, and longing. Negative memories will increase your anger, disappointment, and despair. The last thing you need is to have a good day at work and then get slapped in the face with a reminder of your breakup the moment you step inside your home. If you're not ready to let go of these things completely, put them in a box and hide them somewhere you will not come across until you've healed.

3.) Keep perspective.

Often when we experience emotional pain, things can get blown a little out of proportion in our minds. Catastrophic thinking can take a bad situation and turn it into a disaster of epic proportions. You may find yourself thinking or saying things like "I'll never love again", "I'll never be happy again", or "I've wasted so much time on this. Now it's too late to ever move on" etc. When you're going through the healing process it's important to remind yourself to gain perspective regularly. Think of your situation in the grand scheme. Create a backdrop that will help you keep your thoughts realistic and truthful. Think about how you'll feel about this situation ten or twenty years. Think about other times you've felt low because of a loss or a breakup and take note of how you feel about that now. Recognize that you have healed before and you will heal again. This breakup is not the end of the world. It is merely one of life's many peaks and troughs. You are hurting now but you won't hurt forever. Life will go on.

4.) Be happy about the times you shared together.

When you're going through a breakup it's common to get stuck focusing on the negative. You may experience bouts of intense anger and resentment. You may find yourself calling this a "failed relationship" or a "waste of time". Feelings like these are only natural. Unfortunately, indulging in this way of thinking too much can have adverse effects. It could make you feel bad about yourself and your prospects for the future. Dwelling on the negative can make you feel getting into a relationship with your ex was a bad idea and this could put you off taking risks later in life. Negative thoughts can make you feel like you're not capable of having a lasting relationship and these thoughts can eventually make you bitter, resentful, or cynical. It is important to remember that the fact that your relationship didn't last forever doesn't mean that there were no positive things about it. If your ex brought out a good side of you that's a good thing! If you learned something about yourself or you've grown as a person, you still own those things.

The times that you were happy, satisfied, and excited are things worth remembering with fondness. Experiencing love is a good thing whether or not it stays with you forever. Remind yourself that you haven't wasted time. If you enjoyed the time you shared with your ex, that will always be a time in your life when you felt good. Remember these things if you find yourself feeling overly negative. Love doesn't have to last forever in order to be a good thing. Love is food for the soul no matter who it comes from nor how long it lasts.

5.) Reflect on your personal growth.

Reflecting on your personal growth is a very positive thing you can take out of your experience with your ex. Think about what you learned from your relationship. Think about things you learned about yourself, other people, and the world itself. Think about who you were before your relationship and who you are now. What positive things can you take from this experience that might be useful in the future? What things are possible now that weren't possible before?

Have you changed in ways that you are proud of? Have you learned about a personal fault that you would like to grow past? Have you learned things about other people that will be useful in later relationships? Use your relationship as a learning process and take your new knowledge and your personal growth into your future.

6.) Be yourself.

If you've broken up after being in a relationship for a long time, you may feel like you've lost your "other half". Being on your own can be a huge shock to the system. If you're used to spending every waking hour with someone else, you might forget how to be alone and that can be scary. You might find that a lot of your time is spent thinking about the mere fact that your ex isn't there with you. When you find it hard to be alone - whether you're attending a social event on your own or simply getting ready for bed - remind yourself that being in a relationship doesn't define you. Your ex was not your other half. You are whole with or without them. It's always hard to get into a new routine no matter what the circumstances behind it are, and it's normal to feel scared, confused, or listless in these situations. Focus on the things you love and start remembering who you really are. Don't beat yourself up if you're not sure where to start or if you feel bulldozed by the sudden change.

Go easy on yourself. Allow yourself time to adjust. Let yourself discover new things or rediscover old things you once loved. Listen to music. Indulge in your favorite sport or creative outlet. The world around you might seem big now and it might be frightening to walk into it alone. You can either let it overwhelm you or use it as motivation to get back in touch with yourself and start looking forward to your future.

7.) Smile.

You've heard the saying "laugher is the best medicine" and it may sound crazy but the physical act of smiling can actually increase happiness and decrease negative emotions like fear, sadness, and anger. When you're out in the world - whether you're at work or grocery shopping - smile at the people you meet. At home, watch movies that make you smile. Play with your household pet. Engage in activities that bring you joy. Meet with friends and relatives often and let yourself enjoy their company. It can be hard to do things that make you happy in the aftermath of a breakup but it gets easier with practice. This isn't an easy time and you may feel hurt for a while but it's important to let yourself have a break from your pain from time to time.

8.) Allow yourself to grieve.

Grief is one of the most difficult things we face in life. Coping with loss can be exhausting and it may lead to depression, isolation and self sabotage. One of the hardest things about the grieving process is that it varies from person to person and there is no right or wrong way to experience it. Some people recover from loss quickly and easily, others may grief incredibly difficult to cope with. Where grief is concerned, no two people are the same. This is especially true for the grief of breakups. No one on earth has experienced your relationship apart from you and your ex. This experience is unique and it's yours. Your family or friends might expect you to feel better sooner than you actually do. They might put a lot of pressure on you to "get over it". The fact is, you might feel better in a couple of weeks or you might continue to feel pain for considerably longer than that. You might feel angry, confused or blindsided. You might feel numb or the opposite of numb. You might suffer in silence or you might scream and cry. Grieving isn't easy but it's important to let yourself go through it. Suppressing your grief can make it last longer and could make you feel worse in the long run.

Go easy on yourself during this time. Don't beat yourself up if you still experience sadness when you think you "shouldn't". Be careful not to allow your pain rule your life but do allow yourself to feel it when it comes up. Your feelings just want to be felt. Let them come like waves, recognize them, feel them and then let them go. Eventually the tide will recede and each wave will be more and more tolerable.

9.) Slow down your thinking.

If you have a tendency to overthink things you might notice that your thoughts are racing from one thing to the next without giving you a chance to actually process anything. You might find that your thoughts are jumping rapidly from things you miss about your ex to how you're going to pay the rent to replaying the last conversation you had with your ex to what happens if you run into them at the store etc, etc, etc. If you found that last sentence maddening yet familiar, you know what I'm talking about. Learning to slow your thinking down is a very important skill to have in life. It will help you get through your breakup and it will be useful in other avenues of life as well. Slowing your thinking down is about recognizing when your thoughts are getting the better of you, prioritizing them and regaining your focus. This is important for your attention span and your emotional well being. Learning to effectively slow your thoughts will help you work more efficiently, think more clearly, and sleep better.

There are a number of things you can do to quiet your racing thoughts. Practicing meditation is one of the most effective ways of doing this. You can go to mediation classes to learn how or use a guided meditation recording at home. But if mediation isn't your thing don't worry! When you notice your mind racing, try writing a list of things to think about. Attack your list like any to-do list but only let yourself think of one at a time and put a limit on how long you want to spend on each topic. When you reach your time limit or you come to a conclusion about something, cross it off the list. Conquer practical things first. If you need to write up a new budget now that you're single or figure out how to return your ex's belongings to them without getting roped into an emotional conversation, make a plan and stick to it. Once you've got a good plan of action in place move on to the next topic. If you find yourself thinking about something you've already crossed off the list, be smart and STOP IT.

There is no reason to allow yourself to obsess over things that are aggravating you. Remind yourself that you've already thought about it and you've already come to a conclusion. The next time that thing comes up in your thoughts - whether it was a practical task or an emotional worry - tell yourself that you don't need to think about it anymore. You've dealt with it already.

10.) Confide in someone safe and let it all out.

We all need a chance to get things off our chest when the going gets tough. Talking things through can be extremely helpful in an emotional sense as well as in practical ways. One thing to keep in mind when confiding in someone is only choose to confide in someone you deem to be "safe". This means not only talking to someone who will keep it to themselves but also only talking to people who will respect your feelings and be supportive. Choosing the wrong person to confide in might cause you added pain and frustration rather than making you feel better. If you have friends or family member that you know won't make you feel better, don't talk to them about things that are this close to your heart. We all have people in our lives that we love and appreciate but who can also be overly critical or rude. There's no need to stop being close to these people! Just guard yourself carefully. Talking about your pain is difficult and you deserve to be heard by someone who will be understanding and helpful.

11.) Remember WHY you broke up.

There may be times after your breakup when you feel a desperate desire to get back together with your ex. It's possible that you might feel this way the entire time you're grieving. These feelings are not easy to deal with. You could feel devastated over the loss. You might feel like you've hit rock bottom. You might be experiencing a major struggle. When feelings like this are at their worst, try to think about why you and your ex actually broke up. True, you may have loved each other dearly and you might've hoped to spend the rest of your life with them but there was something that wasn't quite right and remembering what that thing is a good way to put a halt on your pain. If you were the one that broke the relationship up, remind yourself why you did so. What was it about the relationship that wasn't working for you? If you were the on the receiving end of the breakup, think about why. And I don't mean thinking about why *you* weren't right for your ex! I mean for you to think rationally about what was really going on. Was there something lacking between the two of you? Was your ex not ready for a serious relationship? Did they lie or cheat? If your breakup was mutual, what was it that was keeping the two of you from staying together? What was wrong?

Rehashing these things might be difficult at times but it may also help to keep your thinking and actions rational. If you feel like you want to get back together with your ex, ask yourself why. Are the reasons for the breakup no longer there? Or is it simply the fact that you miss your ex and you wish none of this ever happened? Do you want to get back together because you simply don't want to be in pain anymore? Although there are times when two people break up for the wrong reasons and eventually get back together, usually a breakup is a sign that something is wrong. You deserve to be in a relationship with someone who loves and respect you as much as you love and respect them.

12.) Write about it.

In the aftermath of a breakup keeping a journal can really help you make sense of your feelings. Writing things down is a good way to get them off your chest. It's easier to process things once they're laid out in front of you. When journaling, you never need to read the things you write again. In fact, you can write it and tear it up. It's the act of writing that's the healing part. Get the words out of you and then let yourself be done with them.

Another great way to use writing as a healing tool is by writing a letter to your ex. Express your true feelings, your hopes, desires, and fears. Express your anger and confusion. **Do not send this letter.** This is not a chance to tear your ex to shreds or give them power over your! It's a chance to write down everything you would say to them if you could, everything you want to scream and shout at them without damaging your integrity or purposely causing another person pain. When you're finished writing the letter tear it up, burn it, or send it to yourself to dispose of later. Let yourself feel released from your pain and resentment.

13.) Allow yourself to be angry.

Anger can be an extremely difficult emotion to process. Whereas some people can process their anger easily, many people struggle to even admit it when they feel anger. They might find their anger ugly or unjustified. In circumstances like this, many people punish themselves because they feel bad about being angry. Other's become erratic and uncontrollable because of it. It can be hard to know what to actually *do* with anger and it can be easy to become overwhelmed by it.

Anger in itself is not a *bad* emotion. It can be difficult to handle but you're justified in feeling angry at the end of your relationship. Anger is a big player in breakups. You might be angry at your ex and that's okay. You might be angry at yourself, and if you believe you really did did something wrong, that's okay too. You might just be angry at the situation. This is okay. Just be honest to yourself when you're angry. Anger is dangerous when it's not expressed properly. Stifling your anger for long periods of time could lead to bitterness and cynicism. If you don't listen to your anger you're likely to bottle it up now and explode later. It's important to recognize your anger before it gets too big for you to handle.

There is no quick fix for anger but one thing's for sure: ignoring it does not make it go away. If you need to cry and shout or take some energy out on a punching bag, do it. As long as you are careful not to hurt yourself or someone else, anger is better out than in. Tell yourself that you're allowed to be angry. Tell a friend or family member that you're angry. Write it down on a piece of paper. Just get it OUT of you, don't stuff it further inside.

14.) Focus on the things you have.

When you're feeling low it's easy to think about all the things you don't have. In fact, when you're coping with a loss it can seem like the things you don't have have multiplied tenfold! You might hear yourself listing (to friends or in your head) everything you still haven't accomplished or rhyming off all the reasons you're unloveable. You might compare yourself to other people and beat yourself for being "different" than them. This type of thinking is toxic. Thinking about the things you don't have is simply a way of punishing yourself. The pain of your breakup is hard enough! Don't add extra pain by focusing on other negatives. Instead, try to recognize what you *do* have and what accomplishments you *have* achieved. Remind yourself that other people's lives always look pretty on the outside. Comparing yourself to other people is a nonsensical waste of time because you can't hear other people's thoughts!

You don't know what anyone else's true feelings are or what their life is really like. One of the best ways to get focus on the things you *do* have is to recognize when your thinking is venturing into unsafe territory and take 5 minutes to list 5 things that are good in your life right now. After that, list 5 things you like about yourself. This exercise can seem silly and might prove to be extremely difficult but believe it or not, doing it can have an immediate positive effect on you! Put your disbelief aside for a moment and try it. If you feel like you *can't* do it, have a friend force you to. I promise, you can.

15.) Treat yourself like a friend.

If you have a tendency to be a little too hard on yourself, you might be prone to treating yourself badly after your breakup. If you're regularly putting yourself down or getting angry at yourself for feeling upset, stop it! Think of yourself like a friend. How would you treat a friend in the same situation? Would you ridicule them or comfort them? Would you tell another person to wise up and get over it or would you listen to their feelings and be understanding? If you're prone to beating yourself up, remind yourself to treat yourself like a friend. Be understanding with yourself. Treat yourself with nice things. Be gentle and patient with yourself. You don't need enemies right now!

16.) Point your energy in the right direction.

In the midst of a breakup it can be hard to get your head on straight. Often we're so blinded by the pain of our loss that we focus more energy on the our ex than we do on ourselves. If you're used to thinking about other people first it's important to learn how to direct your energy inward. Trying to fix your ex or cure them of their problems is a waste of time. Trying to get them back or convince them that you should be together is almost always a useless and exhausting pursuit. More than anything, the more you focus your attention on your ex, the less you're focusing on yourself and your needs. It can be very very hard to let go of a relationship. You probably believed you and your ex had a promising future future and it hurts terribly to have that idea taken away. But now is a time for you to think about yourself and prioritize your needs. The end goal now should be about making *you* happy.

17.) Recognize your relationship patterns and break your bad habits.

Does this breakup look a lot like other breakups you've experienced? Do you have similar patterns where friends and family are concerned? One of the best things you can do for yourself during this time is identify patterns in your relationships. When it comes to relationships, a lot can be said for self awareness. Studies show that most, if not all, humans have relationship patterns that directly relate to their upbringing and the relationship they had with their primary caregiver as a child. This is not to say that every relationship you have will look exactly like the one you had with your mom or dad. Nor is it to say that what happened in this relationship was necessarily your fault. On the contrary, taking the time to look into any negative patterns you might have is the first step to overcoming them. Remember, it took two people to breakup this relationship. It's not all on you. Your ex will have their own patterns to think about, but let them worry about that.

Before you attempt to begin a new relationship or try to rekindle things with your ex, take some time to explore yourself and how you behave in relationships. Ask yourself why you behave in these ways. Do you regularly seek relationships with people who are unattainable? Do you seek out people who are vulnerable? Do you often go out with people who need to be "parented"? Do you often play the role of caretaker? Or scapegoat? Do you often get taken advantage of? Are there things about your relationship with your ex that were similar to other relationships in your life? If so, are they bad things or good things? Taking the time to really think about these things will help you understand your breakup better and it'll be a big help in any future relationships you have.

Gaining more self awareness can also help you understand current relationships you have with friends and family.

18.) Don't forget about all the other fish!

Although you may not be ready to think about starting a new relationship now, it's important to remember that when you are ready to put yourself back out there, there are a LOT of fish in the sea. It doesn't always feel that way; especially when you live in a small town or you've had an intense connection with someone that you thought would going to last forever. But it's true. There are more people out there than you think and many of them will match with you. Believe that. You may have hundreds of soul mates in the world that you haven't even met yet. This is not the end of your life and it is not the end of love. There is hope. There are still opportunities yet to be discovered. Life doesn't have to end just because this chapter has. You will love again. Just give it time and don't fight it.

19.) Remember that time heals all wounds.

It might be hard to believe right now but you will recover from this. Right now, it may seem like you never will but this heartache will not last forever. Think back to other times you were hurting. Do you still feel pain that you felt five years ago? Do you still feel sad about your high school sweetheart? Probably not.

Remember how sad you felt about those things at the time. This relationship won't have been the same as your high school sweetheart but loss and pain are a part of life and chances are you have felt like this before. Remind yourself that you have hurt before and you have overcome pain before. It might be hard to believe but studies have shown that human beings are at their strongest when they are suffering. This won't be easy but there will come a day when you wake up and find that the world is a brighter place again. Have patience with yourself.

20.) Take a break.

If you're experiencing serious emotional trauma, consider taking a break from work or other obligations. Say no when people ask you for favors if you don't have the energy to do them. Get away for a couple days or cancel everything and go take a long walk in the forest. Let yourself feel your feelings. Let yourself be weak. Take some time to rest. Take a bath. Be quiet. Take time to breathe and just be. By letting yourself face your problems head on, you can overcome them more quickly than if you stuffed them down and tried to ignore them.

21.) Think about how your life will be better.

Times are hard right now and it might be difficult to find a "bright side" to your break up. However, your mood will benefit from some positive thinking from time to time. A good exercise to help get your thoughts focused in positive ways is to take a moment to think about ways your life might improve as a result of the breakup.

Are there things you'll be able to do that couldn't do before? Will you be free in ways you weren't before? Will there be new opportunities for you? New obstacles to conquer? Will you continue to learn and grow? Will you have less turmoil in you life? Fewer disagreements? New and exciting experiences? Write a list of things you'd like to do that you couldn't do while in your relationship or write a list of things you're looking forward to. Exercises like this can feel a bit uncomfortable but they work.

22.) Practice acceptance.

Part of the reason breaking up can be so hard is because you're faced to finally accept that your relationship has ended. This can be truly devastating and can send you into fits of denial and false hope. It's natural to shy away from the truth of the situation, to hope for a resolution or to feel emotionally knocked down. However, it is important to recognize when a relationship is worth fighting for and when it isn't. If the only way for you and your ex to make it work is by having one (or both) of you change in big ways, chances are you're better to walk away from it. Remind yourself of the things you can and cannot change. You must know now that you cannot change another person. No matter how much you understand them, no matter how much you love them or they love you, you can't change them. Accept that your ex is something entirely out of your control.

Now look to yourself. What is it that you or your ex would want you to change? What parts of you can you alter without losing yourself? Is your ex asking more of you than you can realistically achieve? How much sacrifice are you willing to make for this relationship? No matter how much it hurts to let yourself walk away from your breakup, it's vitally important that you accept who you are and who your ex is. Accept the things you cannot change and let yourself move forward.

23.) Keep your "wildness" in check.

During your post breakup time try to do everything in moderation. Going out with your friends is good for you. Being social and blowing off steam is great, but don't drink too much or take drugs. Drink and drugs can lower your mood in the long run and might lower your inhibitions too much. This could obviously result in you doing things you wouldn't do if you were in your right mind. Be careful of getting swept away with partying. Don't party so much you end up losing your job or become flippant. Don't try to sleep with as many people as possible. **Avoid excess of anything.**

You are fragile right now and it's easy to get carried away with "replacement" activities. Be careful about making drastic changes to your appearance or your lifestyle. While you may think that your ex will be intrigued when they see your new tattoo and party pics online, they'll probably be more concerned for you and a little put off by your new "wild side". Remember: dignity and poise are much more admirable and attractive qualities than desperation and a bad attitude.

24.) Ask your friends and family to avoid talking about your ex.

If you're finding it particularly hard to talk about (or listen to other people talk about) your ex, be assertive with your friends and family about it. A lot of times the people close to you think they're being helpful by badmouthing your ex, talking excessively at you about how much they never liked your ex in the first place, or even asking how you're doing too much. It can be really hard to tell the people close to us that, even though we know they care, they're being tactless. If you find it hard to assert yourself to the people closest to you remind yourself that this is your life. You have to protect yourself. Politely ask your family to change the subject. Tell them that you're just not up for talking about it yet. You might feel uncomfortable at the time but it's better than becoming more upset about your breakup than you already do.

25.) Keep your faith in humanity.

After a breakup the world can seem pretty bleak. When you love someone and you're forced to let them go for whatever reason, it hurts. When you trust someone and they let you down, it can be devastating. When the person you respect more than anyone else turns out to be someone who causes you heartache and loneliness, it's hard to imagine ever giving yourself over to someone else again. You are hurting and it's natural to be scared of being vulnerable with another person. You might want to distance yourself from other people altogether and that's fine for a while. But don't give up on love and don't think badly of everyone else on earth because of this one person. This experience is its own thing. It isn't a representation of all relationships and it isn't the end of life as you know it.

Remember that there is a lot of good in people and it can be blissful when you find it. Believe that there is a lot of good in this world. Otherwise you risk becoming cynical and more isolated later in life. If you made a mistake, let yourself try again. If you made a bad decision, give it another go. If someone let you down, that's their problem. It's not indicative of everyone on Earth.

Part Three: Get Your Mind Off Your Breakup

Sometimes, no matter how much positive thinking you employ or how many philosophical debates you have with yourself, you still just can't stop thinking about your ex. You've gotten rid of all the reminders you possibly can, you've blocked them from your social media feeds and you're avoiding any possible triggers but you're still getting flashbacks from time to time. You might know 100% that you don't want you ex back but you still can't help that when you're lying in bed at night or eating breakfast you still get an unwanted emotional sting from time to time. This is to be expected and these things will take some time to get out of your system. There will be things you will always remember and you may always feel a tiny bit of longing for what you once had. This is normal.

However, sometimes the problem is that you've got too much time on your hands and what you need is a good uplifting distraction. This last section is all about what you can do to keep your mind away from painful reminders. You need - and deserve - a break from your pain. Your breakup does not define you. If you feel like you're being swallowed alive by post breakup blues it's time to do something to get your mind off it! Anytime you're finding it hard to get your mind away from negativity, refer to this list and give yourself a break.

1.) Be kind to yourself.

Taking good care of yourself is of upmost importance when you're hurting. You deserve to feel loved and appreciated and with your ex now out of the picture you might not realize that *you* have the power to do this for yourself now. Being kind to yourself means actively doing things to soothe yourself. Do nice things for yourself like buying yourself flowers or treating yourself to a new book. Take yourself out to the movies or let yourself relax in a bubble bath. Go get a massage or watch soppy movies on repeat. Eat well. Give yourself a facial. Get plenty of rest. Do anything that sends a positive message to yourself. Anything that says "I care about me". Your heart will thank you for it.

2.) Tackle your to do list.

Being busy is good for keeping your mind off the breakup and getting refocused at a time when your thoughts and moods are as scattered as a deck of cards caught in a tornado. Most of us have a long list of things that need done or that we'd like to finish (or have been meaning to finish for a long time). Got something that's been on your to-do list for *years*? Now is the time to get it done. What about that stuff you've been meaning to bring to the dump? How about that paint job in your spare room you started but never finished? Bills need paid? Car needs cleaned?

Checking things off your do-do list helps you get closure at a time in your life when you can really benefit from it. Increasing your productivity is great for your self esteem as well as your feelings of independence, self sufficiency, and accomplishment. There's no better time to get stuck in than now.

3.) Hang out with friends.

One of the first things (and the worst things) people tend to do after a breakup is become antisocial. You may feel like you need to batten down the hatches and avoid facing the world for while. The idea of going back to work after a break up can be terrifying. You might feel embarrassed or ashamed. You may find it hard to concentrate, to think or talk about anything else. You might not want to look people in the eye or be forced to put a brave face on when you'd rather stay under the covers until the storm passes. But being antisocial can be very harmful. It can make you feel more alone and can encourage even more negative thought patterns.

Going out and facing the world might be hard, but it will help in the long run. Being in the presence of others gives you a chance to take a break from your thoughts. If you don't want to talk about your situation or you don't want to talk at all, you can simply listen to other people talk about their lives for a while or have a quiet coffee with a friend who respects your current situation. Socializing and feeling a sense of community with others is one of the quickest routes to happiness in human beings.

Whether we're experiencing pain or celebration, the presence of others makes us realize that we aren't alone. You are not the first person to experience loss or sadness. Find comfort in that thought. You aren't alone.

4.) Keep busy.

When you're in the process of getting over a breakup it's important to keep your body and mind from becoming idle. Being busy is a great weapon against post-breakup sadness. Not only does it keep your mind off your ex, it can also mean being productive. Let yourself get consumed with your work. Give your full attention to the things you're passionate about. Start making plans and steps to achieve your personal hopes and dreams. Keeping busy naturally harvests positive thinking. Checking things of your to-do list can give you a nice little boost of satisfaction and confidence. By being productive you're sending a very positive message to yourself, one that says "I'm still me, I'm still alive, and I'm doing just fine. The world is mine for the taking!"

5.) Start a project.

After a breakup it can be really hard to keep your thoughts from wandering into dangerous territory. Negative thinking and ruminating can be damaging to your emotional wellbeing, not to mention how much it can hold you back from enjoying your life. You might find that you have trouble concentrating or you may experience bouts of anxiety and racing thoughts. Being able to steady your mind and keep harmful thought patterns from hurting you is vital to moving on and keeping your spirits up. One of the best ways to quiet your negative thoughts and get refocussed is by starting a project. This can be anything from returning to an old hobby to organizing that cupboard that's been bothering you for months!

Start something crafty, paint your bedroom, write that novel you've been talking about for years! Doing something that requires your undivided attention is a great way to gain control of your thoughts and get your mind off your ex. When you're finished with your project you'll have something to be proud of too!

6.) Do the thing you didn't do in your relationship.

We all have things we wanted to do before or during our relationship that we never got around to actually doing. Maybe you and your ex talked about taking a trip to Paris or perhaps you've wanted to get involved in a community project or take up a new hobby that you couldn't fit into life with your ex. If there are things like this that you've held yourself back from for whatever reason, what better time to do them than now? You are in charge of your life now. You're allowed to make decisions and try new things and nothing can hold you back!

7.) Sing at the top of your lungs!

It might sound cheesy and perhaps a little cringeworthy but there are very few things that feel as good as howling at the moon. Who cares if you sing out of key? Turn on your favorite albums and let yourself wail! Singing loudly can be as cathartic than crying but it can have a much more positive effect on you. Close the curtains and let yourself have a living room dance party. Get all your emotional tension out of your body. The louder the better!

8.) Have a movie marathon.

Now that you've finally got control of the remote you've got a chance to watch all the things your ex never wanted to! Spend the whole day under a blanket, eat a bowl of popcorn and some ice cream and let relax in front of the television. Watch whatever makes you feel good and really let yourself get immersed in the story. Movies offer you two hours of freedom from your thoughts. Take it any chance you get. Just be careful that you choose the right type of movies. Steer clear of movies that are romantic or exceedingly sad. Don't kick yourself while you're down! Choose movies that are inspiring, funny or thought provoking. Choose something that will make you feel good about yourself and the world we live in.

9.) Read.

When was the last time you got enough peace and quiet to read a whole book in a day? Literature is one of the most pleasurable ways to escape the real world and since it occupies your mind, hands, and eyes, it's the best thing for distraction from your troubles. Reading something that you enjoy, whether it's a classic novel or a tabloid magazine is a great way to unwind and get your mind thinking about something else. After a breakup your mind can become exhausted with the flurry of thoughts and emotions coursing through you. Reading will help you switch off and give your brain some much needed rest and relaxation. Becoming immersed in fantasy is just what the doctor ordered.

10.) Learn something new.

It may seem like a cliche but learning new things can have a profound effect on your overall happiness. Not only will it keep your mind off your ex but learning also increases your ability to focus and stimulates curiosity. Learning a new skill can cause a direct increase in your self confidence and help you cope with difficult times. What's more, if you decide to take a class and you're learning something in a group which means you're also being social and meeting new people. It's a win win. Whether you take up French or juggling, flower arranging or football, learning something new is a great way to make a positive change when you need it most.

11.) Volunteer.

Volunteering to work for charity or joining a befriending service for the elderly or people in need can do wonders for your outlook on life. Studies have proven that there are direct connections between having a healthy sense of community and the individual experience of happiness. Furthermore, there is an innate need to feel useful within the human psyche. Getting involved with a cause you believe in could prove to be extremely helpful at this time in your life. Breakups can make us feel lonely and often we don't realize that being surrounded by friends, family, and likeminded people is just as important as having a lover. You might not feel the same connection with a friend that you felt with your ex but it's important to recognize that you aren't alone. All relationships have value. Volunteering can help you connect with others while offering a healthy perspective on your problems.

12.) Rearrange your furniture.

There's a lot to be said for having a change of scenery when times are tough. The good news is that you don't have to go far to get that! Make a big change in your home by moving things around and creating a space that's entirely your own. Have you always hated where your ex threw their dirty clothes? Well now that space is free for you to do whatever you want with it. What about your bedroom? If being in bed is reminding you of intimate times with your ex, rearrange your bedroom, paint the walls a new color, or hang up new art on the walls. Creating new surroundings will help you feel independent, rejuvinated, and more positive about your future.

13.) Buy new bedding.

Sleeping in the same bed you once shared with your partner can be a painful reminder of the intimate times you shared together. It may seem trivial but subtle reminders like this can be just as painful as walking by the place you shared your first kiss. Buy new bedding that you love and think about it as a new beginning. Throw your old bedding away and don't think twice about it! Being free of that one reminder can help you feel lighter, brighter, and more independent. You'll probably find that your quality of sleep improves too.

14.) Spoil yourself!

Now that you don't have a partner to spend all your money on, why not treat yourself? Take yourself out on a spa day, buy some of your favorite treats or your favorite flowers. Make yourself breakfast in bed. Do anything that sends a positive message to yourself; one that says you are loved and appreciated.

15.) Think about the things you didn't like about your ex.

I don't recommend negative thinking often but if you hear yourself talking or thinking about all the wonderful things about your ex and how they could do wrong, you really have to snap yourself out of it. Wallowing in how perfect your ex was is not going to help you get over them. First of all, no one is perfect. No matter how much you try to convince yourself, your ex has flaws. Try not to let your pain cloud your judgement. If you're finding it hard to get rid of all those fantastical beliefs about your ex, every once in a while try to remember the things you didn't like about them when you were together.

Don't think about the big things, those are best left in the past. Think about the little things. All the tiny little things that got on your nerves. The sound of them chewing, how they never did the dishes properly and you always had to rewash them, how they acted like an idiot in public, how they never let you be in charge of the stereo, how they could never concede to being wrong… anything that will take you out of your fantasy world and bring you back to earth.

16.) Be creative.

Creativity is one of the best cures for breakup pain. And whether you believe it or not, being creative is something everyone can do. You don't have to be Picasso or Tchaikovsky to get pleasure out of being creative. Painting, pottery, writing poetry, playing the guitar, baking, sewing… these are all things that anyone can do. You don't have to show what you create to the world! You can keep your projects to yourself or even throw them away when you're finished. There are no rules where art is concerned so let your mind open and get those creative juices flowing. Creativity is a fantastic outlet for your feelings whether you believe that you're "talented" or not.

17.) Spend time with your family.

Being in the company of people you love and trust is beneficial to you no matter what's going on in your life. Having people to talk to, be silent with, and get hugs from is just what the doctor ordered right now. Whether your family includes sixteen siblings, thirty-two cousins, six dogs, and a cat or is simply a handful of close friends is irrelevant. Family are those people who accept, respect and understand you. They're the people that want the best for you and the ones who know just the right thing to say when you're going through a hard time. Reach out to your family (or your chosen family). Organize a get together or invite them to your place for a cup of tea and a chat. These people are a valuable resource right now and they'll be happy to help. All you have to do is reach out!

18.) Write a list of things you're looking forward to.

As I've mentioned before, writing lists can feel a little bit strange but it can be a very helpful practice when your mind is spinning or sinking into negative thoughts. Right now you might not be able to think of the future in a positive light. You might find it hard to even plan what you're going to do tomorrow, but that's why list writing works so well. When you write things down you're actively learning, your mind is focused and you can experience unexpected bursts of energy or clarity. Challenge yourself to write a list of five things you're looking forward to. It doesn't matter if it's something as small as a nice breakfast or something as big as a trip around the world. What matters is that you are reminding yourself of positive, happy things to come in your future.

19.) Reconnect with old friends.

You might find that post-breakup you have a LOT of extra time on your hands. Even though you might find it a bit unnerving at the start, having more time is a good thing! Use it to get back in touch with people you haven't talked to in a while. If you've been meaning to catch up with some friends for ages, now's your chance. Write some letters. Make phone calls. Catch up with your old friends over lunch. If you don't want to talk about your current situation, ask them about what's going on in their life to take a little break from your own.

20.) Reflect.

Take time to reflect on your achievements, strengths and capabilities. Think about your good qualities. Reflect on positive things you have done for others and moments when you have exercised perseverance and resilience. Reflect on how far you have come in life and give yourself credit for every obstacle you have overcome, no matter how big or small. Taking time to listen to your thoughts is an important part of processing them. You might feel more inclined to reflect on your relationship and why things went the way they did. This is normal and it can really help you to understand things better and get closure. Just be careful not to allow yourself to indulge in thoughts that make you feel bad about yourself or the world in general. Reflecting should be something you do in order to learn, grow, and move on, NOT something you use as a stick to beat yourself up with.

21.) Eat well.

Taking care of your body by eating healthy foods and avoiding junk foods is really important when you're feeling down. What we eat directly relates to how we feel. Eating a lot of sugary, salty, fatty snacks could zap your energy and increase depressive tendencies. Grieving can be exhausting and your body needs the right fuel during this time. It's important to keep your blood sugar even to prevent major dips in your mood and energy levels. Make sure you're getting plenty of fruit and vegetables, protein and complex carbohydrates. Avoid eating foods with refined sugars. Taking good care of yourself this way won't just mean you'll be physically healthier, it will also increase your self confidence and increase feelings of self worth.

22.) Go outside!

Fresh air and sunshine can do worlds for your mood and your overall wellbeing. Taking a walk through the forest or on a beach could really help to wake up your senses and steady your thoughts. A change of scenery can lift the spirits dramatically. Seeing birds, squirrels or new flowers in bloom can really help you gain perspective. If you feel you don't have the energy to go far from home, sit outside in your garden or on your balcony and get some Vitamin D from the sun. Take in deep breaths of fresh air and meditate on the thought that it is healing your body and mind with every breath.

23.) Exercise.

There has been a ton of research proving the strength of the mind-body connection. Getting regular exercise can have a dramatic effect on your overall happiness while helping you get into shape. Physical exercise stimulates the release of endorphins and can therefore directly enhance your mood. Furthermore, when implementing a regular exercise regime you can expect better sleep patterns, increased self confidence, and higher energy levels. If going to the gym isn't your thing, don't let that hold you back! You can get into a regular workout routine by taking up running or jogging, playing sports with your friends, cycling, or taking a class in aerobics or dancing. Remember exercise can also be a great way to fill in all that extra time you have on your hands now too!

24.) Use daily affirmations and mantras.

There are a variety of publications in print and online that offer quick and effective daily affirmations that can really help lift your spirits when you're feeling down. Breaking up can wreak havoc on your mood and feelings of self worth and - though it may seem strange at the start - using mantras throughout your day can be a life raft when you feel yourself sinking into the sea negative thoughts. Choose a mantra that you find personally helpful. There's no use repeating something over and over if you don't feel like it applies to you! Choose something you believe in. Something simple like, "right here, right now, everything is okay".

Repeating this aloud or in your head will help you get back to the present when your thoughts are beginning to stray into the past or future. Living in the moment will be an invaluable skill to learn at this time in your life. When we're grieving it's very easy to slip into worries and regrets and those are very dangerous states of mind. Worrying about the future and regretting things that happened in the past only serves to keep you from enjoying your life in the here and now. Using a daily affirmation or mantra that will help keep you rooted in the present is a great way to get mastery over your mind.

25.) Take a vacation.

Why not use your breakup blues as incentive to finally book that vacation you've been thinking about for so long? Take yourself on a trip alone or invite your closest friends to go with you. While you're away, allow yourself to take a vacation from your sadness. Leave it behind you and get some distance from it. Whether you prefer a sunny beach or a city of great art and culture, getting away could be wonderful for you. If finances are too tight to go far away, why not just leave town for a night or two and stay at a bed and breakfast? A vacation doesn't have to be extravagant in order for it to be beneficial to you! You deserve a break!

Afterward. Life Moves on.

Breaking up is never easy. No matter who you are or what role you played in your breakup, it's only natural to hurt. No matter how many breakups you've been through or how complicated they were, you can never be fully prepared for another one. Every one of us hurts when love is lost. Every one of us feels fear when the landscape of our lives changes suddenly. Every one of us cries, screams, and shouts from time to time. Every one of us has woken up in the morning and wished for night to fall so that we might speed our way through hard times. But it's important for all of us to remember that life is too short to wish it away. It is true that human beings are actually at their strongest when they're hurting so no matter how weak you may feel after a breakup, you're actually the exact opposite of that.

They say that when you break a bone, that part of your body will become stronger than it ever was once it has healed. The same can be said for emotional heartache. Each time we overcome a period of loss or sadness we build some immunity against it. The older we get and the more grief we experience, the easier we will find it to overcome that pain when we are forced to face it again later in life. Life is full of ups and downs and we must strive to live it to the fullest and not let things like breaking up take away our joy and happiness. We must value ourselves, love and accept ourselves, take a leap from time to time, give ourselves a break sometimes, and keep reaching for the things we want in life. Focus on YOU and you'll see that before you know it, you'll have entered a brand new chapter in life full of new opportunities and experiences.

Be committed to being good to yourself and treating yourself kindly. You deserve it.

Made in the USA
Monee, IL
27 May 2022

97101479R00036